Israel and the Middle East

Our World Divided

Cath Senker

WAYLAND

First published in 2011 by Wayland

Wayland
338 Euston Road
London NW1 3BH

Wayland Australia
Level 17/207 Kent Street
Sydney, NSW 2000

Senior editor: Camilla Lloyd
Consultant: Dr Ben Fortna
Designer: Stephen Prosser
Picture researcher: Kathy Lockley
Maps: Ian Thompson

Picture Acknowledgments: The author and publisher would like to thank the following for allowing their pictures to be reproduced in this publication: Cover: iStockphoto Johan_R (top) and David Silverman/Getty Images (bottom); Eduardo Abad/epa/Corbis: 43; AFP/Getty Images: 36; Sabah Arar/AFP/Getty Images: 35; Anmar Awad/Corbis: 10; Bettmann/Corbis: 8, 12-13; Deco/Alamy: 38; Gaza Press/Rex Features: 26-27; Stephan Gladieu/Getty Images: 21; Ali Haider/epa/Corbis: 20; Atta Hussein/AFP/Getty Images: 9; Marwan Ibrahim/AFP/Getty Images: 34; iStockphoto Joel Carillet: title page and 16; iStockphoto Boris Katsman: 24; iStockphoto Claudia Dewald: 30; iStockphoto Darren Baker: 33; iStockphoto throughout: Ozgur Donmaz; Cynthia Johnson/Time & Life Pictures/GettyImages: 31; Reuters/Corbis: 22; Patrick Robert/Sygma/Corbis: 11; Ron Sachs/Rex Features: 42; Shaul Schwarz/Getty Images: 29; Nati Shohat/epa/Corbis: 19; Shutterstock Images Ken Tannenbaum: 15; Shutterstock images throughout: Nik Nikiz; Javarman; c.; oriontrail; Francesco81; Fotoline; dusan964; Gemenacom; Picsfive; David Silverman/Getty Images: COVER, 18; Uriel Sinai/Getty Images: 40-41; Uriel Sinai/AFP/Getty Images: 6-7; Sipa Press/Rex Features: 17; STR/Reuters/Corbis: 28; Sultan Al Fahed/X01644/X01644/Reuters: 39.

Acknowledgements
The author would like to acknowledge the following sources of information for case studies: p8-9 Eyewitness in Deir Yassin: *Survivors' Testimonies*, alnakba.org; 10-11 quotes from Scholastic Online and Aish.com; 18-19 Havat Gilad, Israeli outpost: 'Jewish settlers say they remain in West Bank on God's orders' by Patrick Moser (AFP, 31 May 2009); 26-7 *Water, Power and Politics in the Middle East* by Jan Selby (I. B. Tauris, 2003); 34-5 *Dark days for Iraq as power crisis bites* by Charles McDermid and Khalid Waleed (Institute for War and Peace Reporting, June 2010); 42-3 Quote from *Bridging the Green Line: The West-Eastern Divan Orchestra* by Molly McParland, www.culturaldiplomacy.org.

British Library Cataloguing in Publication Data:
Senker, Cath.
Israel and the Middle East. -- (Our world divided)
1. Arab-Israeli conflict--Juvenile literature.
2. Jewish-Arab relations--Juvenile literature.
3. Middle East--History--Juvenile literature.
I. Title II. Series
956'.04-dc22
ISBN: 978 0 7502 6571 3

Printed in China

Wayland is a division of Hachette Children's Books, an Hachette UK company.

www.hachette.co.uk

Contents

Chapter 1

Attack on the Gaza flotilla

In May 2010, a flotilla of six ships was making its way towards Israel. On board were hundreds of activists bringing aid to Gaza. The ships carried building materials, electricity generators and school supplies. The campaigners hoped to break the Israeli and Egyptian blockade on the territory, which was designed to put pressure on Gaza's Islamist Hamas government. The activists argued that the blockade was illegal under international law.

The Israelis believed that some of the goods on board, such as cement, could be used to make rocket launchers to attack Israel. Determined to stop the flotilla from reaching Gaza, on 31 May, Israeli helicopters swooped in over the largest ship, the Turkish-owned *Mavi Marmara*, and commandos descended on ropes. Then the confrontation

▲ *An Israeli military boat intercepts a ship from the Gaza-bound aid flotilla, 31 May 2010.*

began. What happened is hotly disputed. According to the Israeli media, as each soldier lowered himself to the deck, activists assaulted him with bats, clubs, knives and slingshots with glass marbles. Panicking, the soldiers asked for permission to use firearms. They fired on activists, killing nine and injuring 30 people.

However, supporters of the activists claimed the Israelis attacked them first. The soldiers started firing immediately when they landed on the deck, killing unarmed and unthreatening people.

The Gaza flotilla incident is just one in the ongoing saga of division in the Middle East, which includes the Arab–Israeli conflict over land and the struggle to control resources.

From peace to war

Before large numbers of Jewish settlers began to arrive in Palestine in the late 19th century, there was little violence there. During the period of Ottoman rule (1517– 1917) Palestinians and some Jewish people co-existed peacefully. Yet the arrival of many Jewish settlers after World War I led to a contest with the Palestinians over land, which included aggression on both sides.

The unrest continues today, as do tensions between Israel and other Middle Eastern countries. The Middle East is always in the news, partly because much of the world's oil supply comes from the region. Events there have an economic impact on the rest of the globe. Also, foreign powers, particularly the USA, have taken military action in the Middle East, and terrorists have attacked Western targets in other areas of the world. Religion is another reason for the spotlight on the region. It is the birthplace of Judaism, Christianity and Islam. Most of the Middle East is Muslim, while Israel, inhabited mostly by Jews, is the only Jewish state. Palestinians are mainly Muslim; some are Christian. Many people around the world have strong feelings about the Middle East because they share a spiritual link to it.

Viewpoints in the media are often polarized for and against Israel. When reading about the region it is crucial to consider who is talking and what their motivations might be. This book explores the divisions in the region and presents opinions as a basis for debate.

Chapter 2

The roots of division

For this book, the Middle East is defined as Israel and its neighbours, the Gulf States, Yemen, Iran, Iraq, Turkey and North Africa. The history of the region helps to explain the divisions of today.

Origins of the Arab–Israeli conflict

In the late 19th century, the majority of Jewish people lived in Russia and Europe. The eastern European and Russian Jews often suffered persecution because of their religion. More than 3.5 million Jews escaped between 1890 and 1929, most to the USA. A small minority joined the Zionist movement, which held that the Jews needed their own independent homeland in Palestine. Many began to settle there.

▲ *Devout Jews praying at the Jewish holy site, the Western Wall, around 1890.*

Palestine was mostly inhabited by Palestinian Arabs. Britain conquered the land in 1917, during World War I (1914–18), having made the Balfour Declaration, promising a future national homeland for Jews in Palestine. Yet the Palestinians also wanted their own independent state. As Jewish immigration to Palestine increased, the hostility between Jews and Palestinians grew. Some Jewish groups also fought the British, using terrorist methods to try to push them out of Palestine.

During World War II (1939–45), 6 million Jews died in the Nazi Holocaust, and the clamour for a Jewish homeland grew stronger. In 1947, the United Nations (UN) said Palestine would be split between the two peoples. It allocated 55 per cent to the Jewish homeland, although the Jews made up only 37 per cent of the population. Civil war broke out and the Jewish forces gained more land. The State of Israel was declared in May 1948, and its Arab neighbours invaded. When the war ended in March 1949, Israel ruled 78 per cent of the territory. Around 750,000 Palestinians fled as refugees to the West Bank and the Gaza Strip, and to nearby Arab countries; about 150,000 remained in Israel.

Case Study

Murder at Deir Yassin

On 8 April 1948, during fighting between Jewish and Palestinian forces, the important Palestinian leader Abd al-Qadir al-Husseini was killed. The following day, Jewish armed groups assaulted the village of Deir Yassin. Abu Mahmoud remembers defending it:

'I was in the village when the Jews attacked....After his [Abd al-Qadir al-Husseini's] death, we took precautionary measures in case anything would happen: We guarded the village until 02.30 the next morning when the Jews started entering the village with the use of spot and search lights looking for our fighters. The Jews closed on the village amid exchanges of fire with us.

Once they entered the village, fighting became very heavy in the eastern side and later it spread to other parts, to the quarry, to the village center until it reached the western edge. The battle was on three fronts, east, south and north. The Jews used all sorts of automatic weapons, tanks, missiles, cannons. They used [them] to enter houses and kill women and children indiscriminately.'

After a number of similar attacks on Palestinian villages, thousands of villagers fled their homes and land in terror.

▼ *Palestinians gather at the original site of the village in March 2005 to remember the Deir Yassin massacre.*

Arab–Israeli wars

Born through struggle, the State of Israel experienced several other confrontations with its Arab neighbours. Particularly significant was the 1967 war, in which Israel wrested East Jerusalem and the West Bank from Jordan, and the Gaza Strip from Egypt. All had been inhabited by Palestinians. Over time, Israel has made peace agreements with Egypt and Jordan but there has been no resolution with the Palestinians or with Syria or Lebanon.

Israel versus the Palestinians

The division between the Palestinians and Israelis widened as Israel entrenched its dominance over the Occupied Territories (East Jerusalem, the West Bank and Gaza Strip) in the 1970s and 1980s. Israel seized Palestinian land for Jewish settlement, built roads for the settlers and demolished Palestinian homes it deemed to have been illegally built. A minority of extremist settlers claimed that the entire area of Israel and the Occupied Territories belonged to the Jewish people and carried out attacks on Palestinians.

Increasing Palestinian frustration with the failure to regain their land led to the growth of the Palestine Liberation Organization (PLO) against Israel. A minority of Palestinians resorted to terrorist strikes against Israelis. *Intifadas* (popular uprisings) erupted in the Occupied Territories in 1987 and 2000. In the early 2000s, Hamas gained support, offering tougher and more religiously motivated opposition to Israel than the PLO.

Religious division

Linked to the land issue is religion. Israeli and Palestinian territories are holy for Jews, Christians and Muslims.

▲ *Israeli soldiers guard the Muslim Dome of the Rock shrine in Jerusalem. Both Palestinians and Israeli Jews claim the right to govern Jerusalem's holy places.*

Viewpoints

'I don't know if the Jewish temples [in Jerusalem] really existed and were destroyed, but in history we know that Palestine is for the Arabs. We want the holy sites and East Jerusalem to be under Palestinian control. If the Jews want to pray at the Western Wall, they should have access.'

Palestinian Amjad Rafidi, 16,
Al Bireh, Ramallah

'In rewriting the history of Jerusalem each of these [Christian and Muslim] cultures rewrote our place, the Jewish place, in history. They consigned us, they believed, to the dustbin of history...'
'But Jews preserved Jerusalem as a memory... From all over the world we turned and prayed toward Jerusalem...'
'When Jerusalem was liberated... the past became present. What we had longed for became ours.'

Jewish Rabbi Shraga Simmons,
November 2008

▼ *Young Palestinians burn tyres in the street and throw stones at Israeli soldiers during the first* intifada, *1987.*

• Amjad Rafidi is a Palestinian student, quoted on the website of Scholastic, a UK children's publisher.

• The Rabbi Simmons writes for Aish, a Jewish cultural website. He believes the destiny of the Jewish people lies in Israel.

• Consider each writer's background and how this might influence his views.

Timeline: Arab—Israeli Wars

1967
During the Six-Day War, Israel occupies East Jerusalem, the West Bank, Gaza Strip, the Golan Heights and the Sinai Peninsula.

1973
Yom Kippur War: Israel defeats a surprise invasion by Syria and Egypt.

1982
Israel invades Lebanon to crush the PLO.

2006
Israel invades Lebanon after the kidnapping of two soldiers.

Divided over water

The control of resources is a vital element in the Arab–Israeli conflict. The region is arid (very dry) and water is scarce. After 1948, the State of Israel rapidly developed agriculture, and farmers began to grow crops such as citrus fruit, melons and potatoes, which required a lot of watering. Water was also needed for industrial development, and for domestic use, to cater for Israel's fast-growing population as thousands of immigrants made their home in the new nation.

During the Arab–Israeli war of 1967, Israel conquered a vast swathe of territory from its neighbours that doubled its water resources. It gained complete control of the water from the West Bank and the Sea of Galilee, sowing the seeds for battles with the Palestinians over this resource.

Struggle for oil

The discovery of oil in the Middle East also led to hostilities. It was a significant

▼ *A small farming settlement near B'sor, southern Israel, in 1963. The farmers move the irrigation pipe using specially designed wheels.*

reason why Western powers became involved in the region. Oil was first found in Iran and Arabia in the early 20th century. At first, British companies dominated oil production. After World War II, individual countries wanted to nationalize their oil resources so that they could manage them. Yet Western countries often intervened. For example, in 1951 Mohammad Mossadeq became prime minister of Iran and nationalized its oil. In 1953, his elected government was violently overthrown in a coup sponsored by the USA and Britain.

Israel – key Western ally

Some influential politicians in Western countries believed that an alliance with Israel in such a strategic location could help to protect their interests in the region – and the Israeli government agreed. In 1951, the year Iran nationalized its oil, the Israeli newspaper, *Ha'aretz*, spelt this out: 'Israel is to become the watchdog. . . . if for any reasons the Western powers should sometimes prefer to close their eyes, Israel could be relied upon to punish one or several neighbouring states whose discourtesy to the West went beyond the bounds of the permissible.'

Indeed, in the 1967 Arab–Israeli war, Israel overpowered the Arab states, including Egypt, which was trying to free itself from Western influence. In the following years, the USA provided Israel with sophisticated weapons – just as the oil nations were beginning to work together to increase their power.

The Cold War

The intervention of foreign powers in the Middle East was not because of oil alone. After World War II, the Cold War began: political friction began between the USA and the Soviet Union and each side attempted to gain influence over other countries to boost their power. From the 1950s, the communist Soviet Union provided arms and support to the newly independent Arab countries in the Middle East, while the USA was prepared to assist any country resisting communism.

The oil nations unite

In 1960, the oil nations of Iran, Iraq, Kuwait, Saudi Arabia and Venezuela formed the Organization of the Petroleum Exporting Countries (OPEC). Several other countries in the Middle East and elsewhere soon joined. OPEC's aim was to help these nations – many of which had recently achieved independence – to take control of their petroleum industries. This was a mainly economic union, but during the 1973 oil crisis, OPEC countries used oil as a political tool. For several months, they refused to sell oil to countries that had supported Israel in the 1973 Arab–Israeli War.

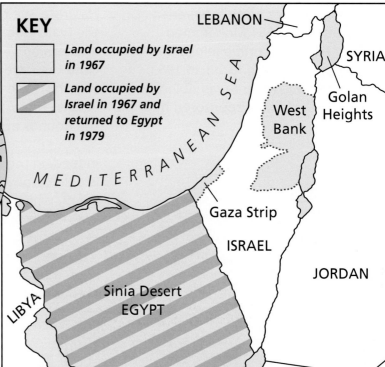

KEY

Land occupied by Israel in 1967

Land occupied by Israel in 1967 and returned to Egypt in 1979

LEBANON
SYRIA
MEDITERRANEAN SEA
West Bank
Golan Heights
Gaza Strip
ISRAEL
JORDAN
Sinia Desert
EGYPT
LIBYA

EUROPE
UK
Iran
Libya
Israel
AFRICA

▲ *Israel's location on the world map.*

▶ *Israel and the territories it occupied in 1967.*

The Middle East Countries

THE GULF STATES:
Saudi Arabia, Bahrain, Qatar, United Arab Emirates(UAE), Oman, Kuwait

NORTH AFRICA:
Libya, Algeria, Tunisia, Morocco

ISRAEL AND ITS NEIGHBOURS:
Lebanon, West Bank, Gaza Strip, Egypt, Syria, Jordan, Iran, Iraq, Yemen, Turkey

CLIMATE:
Hot and dry. A large part of the region is desert. Winters are generally mild with some rain.

POPULATION:
350 million people, of whom about two-thirds are Arabs.
Other main population groups: Persian, Berber, Kurdish, Jewish (5.6 million)

LARGEST CITIES IN THE MIDDLE EAST:
Tehran, Iran; Baghdad, Iraq; Jeddah and Riyadh, Saudi Arabia

▲ *The terrorist attacks on the USA on 11 September 2001 killed nearly 3,000 people.*

Wars over oil

Oil wealth caused division between OPEC members too. A dispute over the ownership of oil-rich areas was a significant factor in the Iran–Iraq war of 1980–88. Soon after, in 1990, Iraq invaded Kuwait. If Iraq had held Kuwait, it would have presided over 20 per cent of the world's proven oil reserves. However, an international military alliance, led by the USA, restored the Kuwaiti government in the 1991 Gulf War. Some political experts have argued that the desire to manage oil resources in Iraq was the main reason for the US-led invasion and occupation of Iraq in 2003. Officially, the aim was to topple Iraq's dictator Saddam Hussein and bring about democracy.

Viewpoints

'I am saddened that it is politically inconvenient to acknowledge what everyone knows: the Iraq war is largely about oil.'

Alan Greenspan, September 2007

'Getting rid of Saddam Hussein was the right thing to do and the world is a better place without him.'

Former US President, George W. Bush, News.com.au, 4 June 2010

• Greenspan was chairman of the US central bank (1987–2006). The quote is from his memoir.

• George W. Bush is the former US president who decided to invade Iraq. The source is an Australian online news service.

• Consider how each person might have formed his views about the war in Iraq.

The rise of Al-Qaeda

During the early 2000s, many in the Middle East opposed what they saw as heavy-handed Western intervention in the region. A tiny minority responded by joining terrorist cells, linked to an international network that became known as Al-Qaeda. They carried out violent actions against US targets, including the deadly attacks on the USA of 11 September 2001.

The Arab–Israeli conflict remains essentially a struggle over territory; both Israeli Jews and Palestinians lay claim to the land of historic Palestine.

A divided land

The Israeli government currently rules Israel within the borders established after the 1967 war, as well as East Jerusalem and the West Bank. In the 1990s, Israel transferred responsibility for Palestinian civilians in the West Bank and Gaza to a Palestinian Authority (PA) but maintained overall rule of the area. In 2005, the government forced Israeli settlers to leave the Gaza Strip. However, Israel still controls access to the territory, so Palestinians claim Gaza remains occupied. The following year, Hamas came to power after winning the elections in Gaza, while the PA, dominated by Fatah (the largest group in the PLO) remained in power in the West Bank. So the Palestinian territories are further divided from each other.

A dividing wall

Israel has separated itself from the West Bank by building a Security Wall. It states that this is necessary as a boundary and a barrier to halt Palestinian attacks on its citizens. However, Palestinians oppose the wall, which they dub the Separation Barrier. It is built on West Bank land and causes them enormous practical difficulties. Many villagers have become cut off from their farmland or olive trees, or their village has been divided or enclosed by the barrier.

▲ *Palestinian villagers rely on Israeli soldiers to allow them to pass through the Security Wall. Yet the soldiers do not always open the gates for them.*

Viewpoints

'The security fence, the buffer zone, and even the sections of the fence which have not been completed, limit the ability of terrorist organizations to enter Israel and present operational obstacles, especially for those organizations active in northern Samaria [the West Bank], making it difficult for them to carry out suicide bombing attacks within Israel.'

Israel Diplomatic Network website

'Israel has the right and duty to protect its citizens from attacks. However, the building of the Separation Barrier as a means to prevent attacks inside Israel is the most extreme solution that causes the greatest harm to the local population ....Even if we accept Israel's claim that the only way to prevent attacks is to erect a barrier, it must be built along the Green Line [the 1967 border between Israel and the West Bank] or on Israeli territory.'

Website of Btselem

• The Israel Diplomatic Network is the Israeli government's official website.

• Btselem is an Israeli human rights organization that informs the public about human rights abuses in the Occupied Territories.

• Both sources are Israeli, but they offer different views on the wall. Consider why their viewpoints might be different.

◀ *In 2005 British graffiti artist Banksy painted murals on the Palestinian side of the wall to focus attention on the issue.*

Timeline

2002
Israel begins building the Security Wall (Separation Barrier).

2005
Israeli settlers leave the Gaza Strip.

2006
The militant Islamic party Hamas wins the elections in Gaza.

2008
Israel invades Gaza in response to increasing rocket attacks from the territory.

2009
Benjamin Netanyahu is elected Prime Minister of Israel.

Jerusalem: conflicting claims

Both Israel and the Palestinians claim Jerusalem as their spiritual capital. In 1948 it was split into West Jerusalem (Israeli-ruled) and East Jerusalem (governed by Jordan). In 1967 Israel conquered East Jerusalem. The holy sites, including the Western Wall, sacred to Jews, and the Muslims' Dome of the Rock shrine, fell into Israeli hands. From the 1980s, Israel began to designate an area of approximately 100 square miles (about 250 sq km) around Jerusalem as 'Greater Jerusalem'; it includes East and West Jerusalem and nearby West Bank neighbourhoods. Israeli Jews have settled in these formerly Palestinian areas.

Competing aims

All these clashes over land arise from different national desires. Israel wants to maintain the country as a Jewish state, since it is the only one in the world. It aims to increase the territory settled by Israeli Jews by continuing to build communities in Greater Jerusalem and the rest of the West Bank. The Palestinians demand a halt to this settlement building. They hope to create their own independent nation. Most would accept a state in the West Bank and Gaza Strip with East Jerusalem as its capital and do not expect to regain all of historic Palestine.

Violence on both sides

Both sides use violence to try to further their aims. From September 2000 to October 2010, Palestinians killed 742 Israeli civilians in Israel, the West Bank and Gaza. In 2008, Gazan militants launched rocket attacks on Israel, which greatly frightened the population,

▲ *Israeli soldiers search for Palestinian militants in the West Bank town of Nablus after an attack on Israeli citizens in Jerusalem, 2003.*

although they caused few casualties. Israel has responded forcefully to attacks on its citizens. For instance, in retaliation for the rocket attacks, Israel launched a massive invasion of Gaza. According to non-governmental organizations (NGOs), the onslaught killed about 1,400 Gazans and devastated government buildings, homes, hospitals and water facilities. As well as direct attacks, the daily violence of the Israeli occupation includes military checkpoints to control the movement of West Bank Palestinians, house demolitions and the detention of large numbers in prison without trial.

Case Study

Havat Gilad, settlement outpost

Most of the 290,000 Israelis in the West Bank live in settlements considered legal by their government but illegal under international law. They have moved for economic reasons and to make their lives more comfortable. A small minority believe they have a God-given right to the whole of Israel and the Palestinian territories and have set up their own outpost communities.

▲ *Jewish settlers in Havat Gilad in July 2010.*

Rabbi Yaacov Savir runs a Jewish religious school in the settlement outpost of Havat Gilad in the West Bank. The outpost is not authorized by the Israeli government.

Yet Savir claims that 'Jewish people live here by Biblical right'. He thinks there is no such group of people as the Palestinians, and that it's the Arabs who want to stop Jewish people from living in their homes. He says the Arabs should find somewhere else to live.

The Israeli government has pulled down very few of these illegal outposts, and even if it did bulldoze Havat Gilad, the settlers would simply rebuild it. As Savir says, '[We] will certainly fight for every millimetre. No one will leave his home.'

Regional strains

The Arab–Israeli conflict involves neighbouring countries too. Many Palestinian refugees who fled in the wars of 1948–9 and 1967 live in nearby lands: about 1.9 million in Jordan, and over 420,000 in both Lebanon and Syria. Antagonism towards Israel exists in these countries because of the presence of a large number of Palestinians who do not belong to the host country yet cannot return to their homeland. The refugees are frustrated because they do not have the same rights as the local population. In Lebanon, for instance, Palestinians are not permitted to work in many professions, to own property or to travel freely.

Rise of Islamism

One response to the failure to achieve peace between Israel and all of its neighbours has been the rise of political Islamism – the belief that reviving Islam is the way to transform society. Islamist parties offer practical help, such as welfare programmes for the population, as well as opposing US influence and Israeli power. For example, the Israeli army occupied southern Lebanon in 1982 to drive out the PLO, which was based there. The Islamist party Hizbullah increased in strength to oppose the Israeli occupation and the State of Israel itself. In 2000, Israeli troops finally left Lebanon. Then in 2006, the kidnapping of Israeli soldiers by Hizbullah triggered renewed Israeli invasion and war.

▲ *An Israeli airstrike on a suspected Hizbullah stronghold in Lebanon, August 2006.*

Hizbullah in Lebanon

Hizbullah is a Muslim political party that emerged in the early 1980s, with financial support from Iran. It aimed to push Israeli forces out of Lebanon. Hizbullah has remained extremely hostile to Israel, saying Israel has no right to exist. It has several seats in parliament and ministers serving in the national government. Hizbullah has gained popular support by providing health care and social services to ordinary Lebanese people.

Hizbullah provides social assistance, education and health services in Beirut, Lebanon in 2006.

Hizbullah was at the centre of the month-long fight against Israel and claimed victory at the end – although at the cost of more than 1,100 Lebanese and 160 Israeli lives, and widespread destruction.

Syria and Iran

Like Lebanon, Syria has never made peace with Israel and is known to host anti-Israeli groups such as Hamas and Hizbullah. According to a report in the French press in 2010, Hizbullah had three units in Lebanon, including training camps for militants.

The Islamic state of Iran also opposes Israel and has offered support to Hizbullah since its formation. Israel has expressed anxiety about the threat from Iran, especially its possible development of nuclear weapons (although Israel itself has built nuclear weapons). In 2008, Israel considered launching a military strike on Iran's nuclear sites, but was deterred by the USA. Any such offensive would undoubtedly lead to retaliation by Iran against Western interests and provoke a serious escalation of violence in the region.

Big powers wade in: the USA

Countries outside the region play a significant role in the Arab—Israeli conflict. The USA is a key ally of Israel, providing economic backing and military support, including hi-tech weapons systems. It provides more aid to Israel than to any other nation in the world: US $3 billion (£2 billion) was allocated for 2011.

Politically, the USA is involved as a peace broker between Israel and the Palestinians and the Arab nations, but has proved unable to achieve a lasting agreement.

The failure to resolve the situation, along with US military intervention in the region since the Gulf War of 1991, has aroused anti-Americanism among many people in the Middle East. They think that the United States shows favouritism towards Israel.

◀ *Two students burn a US flag with a Star of David, the symbol of the Israeli state, on a peaceful march in Cairo, Egypt, in 2002.*

The EU and Turkey

The European Union (EU) has mostly backed US policy in the Middle East. It joined Israel and the USA in imposing sanctions on Gaza after Hamas won the elections in 2006. The EU argues for the establishment of a Palestinian state alongside Israel, but it has strong economic ties with Israel and is reluctant to apply heavy pressure on the Israeli government.

In the early 2000s, Turkey became engaged in Middle East diplomacy, attempting to fill the vacuum left by the failure of US-led peace initiatives. It has established relations with Hamas in Gaza and strongly criticized Israel's military actions in the Palestinian territories. The Turkish government has also developed close ties with Iran and Syria and is working towards progressing negotiations between Syria and Israel. But as of 2010, no major development in Middle East peace had been achieved.

Viewpoints:
United States and the Middle East

How would you describe your attitudes toward the Obama Administration policy in the Middle East?

	2009	2010
Hopeful	51	16
Neither hopeful nor discouraged	28	20
Discouraged	15	63

The Arab Public Opinion Poll, 2010
Numbers refer to people

'Today, the United States and Israel are the closest of friends and allies. During more than four decades of state-building, Israelis have looked to the United States for inspiration, financial and military assistance, and diplomatic support. Americans, in turn, have viewed Israel with a special appreciation for its successful effort to follow the Western democratic tradition, its remarkable economic development, and its determined struggle against its uncompromising enemies.'

Mitchell G. Bard, the Jewish Virtual Library, 2010

• The Arab Public Opinion Poll, 2010 is compiled from interviews in Egypt, Jordan, Lebanon, Morocco, Saudi Arabia and the UAE. When Barack Obama came to power in the USA in 2009, many Arabs hoped his policies would favour them, but they were soon disappointed.

• The Jewish Virtual Library is a pro-Israeli website that aims to strengthen ties between Israel and the USA.

Chapter 4

The water wars

The Middle East is a dry region, and the demand for water outstrips supply. The struggle to dominate water supplies has become a contentious issue between Israel, Palestinians and neighbouring countries.

Israel: fair use of water?

Israel controls the waters of the West Bank and the Sea of Galilee, which it took over after occupying the West Bank in 1967. It manages both the River Jordan and the underground water sources. Israel commands the lion's share of the water; for example, it takes 80 per cent of the West Bank mountain aquifer's flow, while Palestinians receive 20 per cent to supply all their requirements.

Israel asserts that agriculture is important to the economy and its farmers need large quantities of water to irrigate their crops. Nevertheless, it claims that it does not use a larger proportion of the region's water than in the 1950s. Also, Israel points to its successful development of desalination facilities (to remove the salt from sea water) and water-saving techniques. For instance, farmers use drip irrigation, in which water and nutrients flow directly to the area around the plant's root system. This is a highly efficient use of water.

Water for Palestinians

Water is just as important to the Palestinian economy and population. Yet since the West Bank Palestinians do not possess their own water supply, they have to buy water from Israel. The World Bank contends that Israelis consume four times as much water per person as the Palestinians do, although the Israeli government insists it is only twice as much. Gaza's only water source is the Gaza Aquifer, but water quality is a problem. The water has become polluted and salinated (salty), threatening people's health. To make matters worse, during the military attacks of 2008, the water and sanitation systems were damaged. By late 2010, they had still not been repaired because the Israeli blockade prevented the entry of the materials needed to fix them.

▲ *This photograph shows modern agricultural watering irrigation in Israel.*

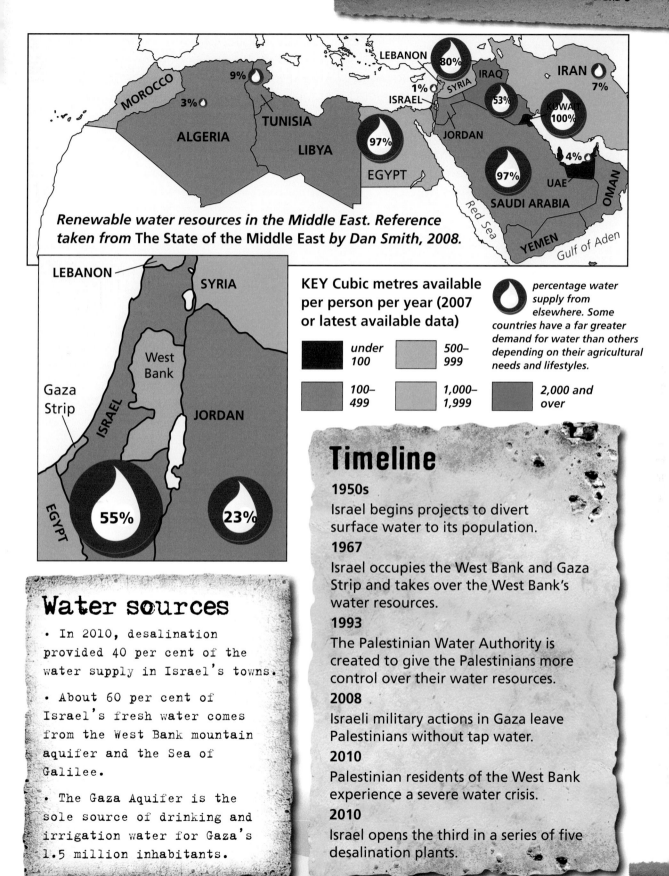

Renewable water resources in the Middle East. Reference taken from The State of the Middle East by Dan Smith, 2008.

KEY Cubic metres available per person per year (2007 or latest available data)

percentage water supply from elsewhere. Some countries have a far greater demand for water than others depending on their agricultural needs and lifestyles.

- under 100
- 100–499
- 500–999
- 1,000–1,999
- 2,000 and over

Water sources

- In 2010, desalination provided 40 per cent of the water supply in Israel's towns.

- About 60 per cent of Israel's fresh water comes from the West Bank mountain aquifer and the Sea of Galilee.

- The Gaza Aquifer is the sole source of drinking and irrigation water for Gaza's 1.5 million inhabitants.

Timeline

1950s
Israel begins projects to divert surface water to its population.

1967
Israel occupies the West Bank and Gaza Strip and takes over the West Bank's water resources.

1993
The Palestinian Water Authority is created to give the Palestinians more control over their water resources.

2008
Israeli military actions in Gaza leave Palestinians without tap water.

2010
Palestinian residents of the West Bank experience a severe water crisis.

2010
Israel opens the third in a series of five desalination plants.

Thirsting for water

Israeli human rights organization Btselem has accused Israel of deliberately denying the West Bank Palestinians much-needed water, although their Israeli neighbours are well supplied. In the summer, there is a higher demand for water from both Israelis and Palestinians. The Israeli water company, Mekorot, steps up the supply to the Israeli settlers but does not increase – or even decreases – the supply to the Palestinians. Mekorot denies Btselem's accusation. It has asserted in the Israeli press that it provides more water to the West Bank than required under a 1993 agreement.

Whether or not Mekorot is meeting its obligations, the lack of water is far more serious in Palestinian villages and refugee camps than in urban areas, causing particular difficulties for farmers. Many communities

are not connected to a running-water network. For example, Jabal Mukabber is a Palestinian village in the West Bank, in the area Israel calls 'Greater Jerusalem'. It has no sewer system and there are frequent water shortages. Yet close by, the new Jewish settlement of Nof Zion has an up-to-date sewer system and water mains. Gardens and swimming pools will be supplied with all the water they need. The Palestinians argue that this is unfair.

Case Study

Coping with water shortages

West Bank Palestinians have devised a variety of methods to access water. Their main source is rainfall, which is plentiful between November and May. They collect it on rooftops and store water in cisterns near their homes. In the summer months, Palestinians fill up jerry cans (petrol cans), plastic bottles and even mini-tankers with spring water – if they are lucky enough to live near a spring. Otherwise they are forced to buy water at inflated prices from private water sellers.

One resourceful villager in the village of Quasiba in the West Bank excavated a cavern behind his home using drills and explosives. He laid rubber tubing from the cavern to tanks on the rooftops of his home and five others. During the winter, the cavern filled with water flowing down from the mountain behind and supplied enough water for the six families' domestic needs.

Palestinians have also learnt to manage with little water, especially in the hot summer months. At times they have to reduce the amount of cooking they do to avoid washing up, or let the laundry pile up until the water is switched on again. This situation can make people feel humiliated. As one woman said, 'you feel like you're not human'.

◄ *A Palestinian boy collects water in Khan Yunis refugee camp, Gaza, November 2007.*

Water as a weapon

The argument is not simply about the fair allocation of water. There is independent evidence that Israel has deliberately depleted the water supply to the Palestinians. The human rights organization Amnesty International has published reports of water in the Occupied Territories being so polluted that it cannot be drunk and can damage the health of livestock.

Israel also imposes restrictions that limit Palestinian access to water resources. It will not allow the West Bank to export water to Gaza even though the water and sewer system there is in crisis. Palestinians say that Israeli restrictions make it hard for them to establish new water projects. When they apply for permission to dig wells or other water installations, they meet with repeated refusals.

However, Israel argues that Palestinian inefficiency is the main problem. Even when it does give permission for new water projects, the Palestinian Authority fails to build them. The Palestinians refuse to recycle their waste water, and the untreated water pollutes the mountain aquifer.

What does each side want?

The water conflict occurs because each side has a different understanding of its rights to water. Israel argues that it has one of the most scientifically advanced agriculture sectors in the world, requiring a consistent water supply. The nation is highly

▲ *Palestinians walk along a street flooded with sewage water in Gaza City in 2008.*

▲ *Israelis enjoy a swimming pool in Tiberias, Israel.*

industrialized and the population has good living standards, which entail heavy water usage – including using swimming pools to cool off in the hot climate. Israel also wants to ensure it has secure water supplies for its growing settlements in the West Bank.

For the Palestinian authorities, the issue of water rights is central. The restrictions imposed by Israel make it extremely difficult to provide water to the population. Also, the authorities are extremely weak. They have to cope with the Israeli occupation, which involves regular closures of transport routes and damage to infrastructure during military attacks. The Separation Barrier cuts off some farmers from their water supply. The Palestinians argue that Israel's unjust water policy should be reversed so that they have fair access to this vital resource.

To the Palestinians, denying access to water is part of Israel's campaign to take more land. As Hafez Hereni, living in a village in southern Hebron, West Bank, comments: 'We spend a lot of money on water and we never have enough. They are trying to force us out of the area by all means. Taking our land is one way and limiting our access to water is another way.'

Water needs

The World Health Organization recommends that each person should have 100 litres of water a day.
- The average Israeli has 300 litres
- The average Palestinian has 70 litres
- Some Palestinians have only 20 litres

(Amnesty International, Oct 2009)

Regional water disputes

Since Israel's establishment, there have been disputes with its neighbours over the water of the Jordan River. The river's basin straddles the territories of five countries: Lebanon, Syria, the West Bank, Jordan and Israel. In 1960, the Arab League planned to divert the water of two tributaries of the Jordan River – the Hasbani River from Lebanon and the Banias River from Syria – to prevent them from flowing into Israel. In 1964 Syria began work on the diversion. Israel reacted by initiating armed clashes, and Syria abandoned the scheme in 1966. The following year, as well as conquering the West Bank and Gaza Strip, Israel seized the Golan Heights from Syria. Before, Syria had enjoyed access to the Sea of Galilee. Since then, all the water has gone to Israel.

The need for solutions

Despite such hostility in the region, water disputes can be solved. As part of the 1994 agreement between Jordan and Israel, the two countries recognized each other's rights to water from the Jordan and Yarmouk rivers and the Araba/Arava ground water. They agreed that water resources were insufficient and that they would cooperate to manage the existing supplies.

Further compromise is desperately needed. In recent years, the overuse of water resources in the region has reached crisis point. Natural fresh water is running low in Israel and the Palestinian territories because of the rising population and low winter rainfall.

▲ *An Israeli fishing boat in the Sea of Galilee.*

The Jordan River valley is endangered. Israel, Jordan and Syria have diverted most of the tributaries of the Lower Jordan River to use for agriculture and domestic use. By 2011 it was expected that parts of the Jordan River would dry up entirely for most of the year. The mountain aquifer, vital for both Israel and the Palestinians, is increasingly under threat from excessive exploitation by Israel and the discharging of untreated waste, mostly by the Palestinians. Cooperative efforts could be made to protect the water supplies and use water more sustainably.

◀ *Prime Minister Rabin and King Hussein of Jordan shake hands as US President Bill Clinton claps, at the signing of the Israel–Jordan peace treaty, 1994.*

Viewpoints

'The water crisis in the Arab world is compounded by growing demand, highly inefficient usage, government corruption, domestic instability and poor management, say international experts, leading to inadequate supply, which could spark domestic hostilities as well as conflict with neighboring countries.'

D. Bloomfield, *Jerusalem Post*, 22 April 2010

'From the Eastern Aquifer, located in the West Bank, Israel takes 37% of the water for the illegal settlements. In some cases, Israel takes water from Palestinian aquifers and sells that water back to the Palestinians at almost twice the price.'

Palestine Monitor website, 19 March 2009

• The *Jerusalem Post* is the most widely read English-language Israeli newspaper and website. The author blames Arab countries for water-supply problems.

• Palestine Monitor was set up by Palestinian writers in 2000 to give a voice to the Palestinians living in the West Bank and Gaza Strip.

Chapter 5

Oil - 'black gold'

Oil is a vital source of energy worldwide. Around 68 per cent of the world's proven oil reserves are in the Middle East, mostly in the Gulf States. The demand for oil is rising rapidly, but the amount available is finite. Therefore, the struggle to control its supply is crucial.

Oil 'haves' and 'have nots'

Several Middle Eastern nations have oil: the Gulf States of Oman, the UAE, Kuwait, Bahrain, Qatar and Saudi Arabia; Iran, Iraq, Yemen and Syria. The Gulf States are experiencing economic growth, benefiting from the high price of oil on the world market. Yet possessing oil does not necessarily lead to economic success. Iraq, for instance, was embroiled in war in the early 2000s, while Yemen was running out of oil and suffered from an extremely weak government. Furthermore, several of the region's nations, such as Israel, Jordan and Lebanon, have no oil resources at all.

The USA and oil

Access to oil, so valuable it is known as 'black gold', is an essential factor in international relations. The USA pays special attention to its relationship with oil producers because it consumes more oil than any other country – 26 per cent of global production – even though it represents only 5 per cent of world population. It could be argued that the USA operates a 'carrot and stick' policy towards oil-rich nations, rewarding its friends and punishing those who oppose it.

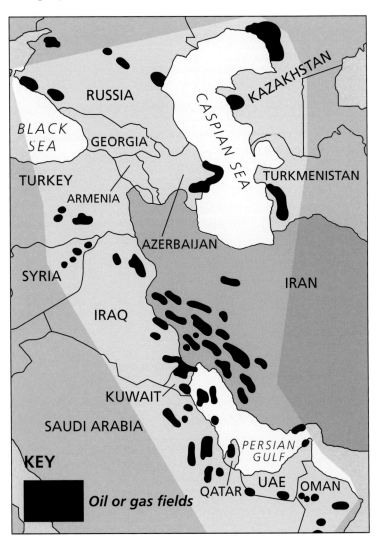

▼ *Most of the world's oil and gas fields are found in the 'oil corridor' in the Middle East.* *Source:* **Asia Times.**

KEY

Oil or gas fields

▲ *Doha is the capital city of oil-rich Qatar.*

The carrot

The USA favours alliances with oil-rich countries to ensure an uninterrupted flow of petroleum. For example, major oil producer Saudi Arabia is a staunch ally. In 2010, the Obama government announced its plan to sell US $60 billion (£38 billion) of weapons to Saudi Arabia – the biggest arms deal in US history. As Andrew Shapiro, from the US political and military affairs department commented, this would 'enhance Saudi Arabia's ability to deter and defend against threats to its borders and to its oil infrastructure, which is critical to our economic interests.' Before going ahead, the USA sought Israel's approval of the deal, making it clear that Israel would still have the military upper hand in the Middle East.

Oil reserves

The world's top ten oil producers and their proven world oil reserves, in billions of barrels:

Saudi Arabia: 264
Canada: 178
Iraq: 143
Iran: 138
Kuwait: 102
Venezuela: 99
UAE: 98
Russia: 79
Libya: 46
Nigeria: 36

The World Factbook, 2010

The stick

The USA is prepared to take action to try to increase its oil supplies. In 1972, Iraq nationalized its oil resources. Yet it was unable to develop petroleum production at a fast pace because of the Iran–Iraq War and, from 1990, economic sanctions – a UN ban on trading with Iraq to put pressure on its dictator Saddam Hussein. In 2003, the US government hoped that by overthrowing Saddam Hussein and bringing in a democratic, pro-Western government would allow Iraq to produce more oil for export. However, the violent resistance to US forces and civil conflict within Iraq in the years after the invasion and military occupation actually lowered the levels of oil production.

Then in 2010, spectacular opportunities arose to increase the flow of oil. New forecasts showed that Iraq's oil production was likely to quadruple over the next decade because its oil is onshore (on land) and easy to access. Global petroleum companies, such as BP and Royal Dutch Shell, rushed to sign deals with the Iraqi government to develop the oil fields. The Iraqi government will receive money from the rise in oil production. It desperately needs this oil income to rebuild the country, including its power stations, which cannot supply enough electricity to the population. Yet the investing oil companies will take a large share of the profits, too.

▲ *Here, an Iraqi resistance group has attacked an oil installation near the northern Iraqi town of Kirkuk, February 2005.*

Case Study

Electricity crisis in Iraq

Iraq has the third-highest reserves of oil in the world, yet many people endure regular fuel shortages. In June 2010, temperatures in the capital, Baghdad, soared above 50° C. Yet owing to electricity shortages, people could not turn on the air-conditioning to bring relief in the baking heat. The government claimed that most Iraqis had electricity for six hours a day, but in Baghdad's poorer neighbourhoods, the supply was available for only one to two hours daily. Not only this, but also the price of electricity had recently doubled.

The electricity issue affected everyone. Thousands of citizens, especially in poorer areas, risked bombings and violence to protest in the streets about the fuel shortages. The police responded brutally to control the crowds; in Basra, in the south, they opened fire on protesters, killing at least two people.

▲ *Iraqis protest about electricity shortages, August 2009.*

Sameh Mohammad, a Baghdad mother of four, expressed common feelings: 'How can an oil-rich country like Iraq not provide electricity for its people? Our oil is enough to build cities and countries, how is it that government can't give us more than one or two hours of power each day? It's been like this for years.'

Timeline

1990
Iraq invades Kuwait and world oil prices rise.

1991
US-led Gulf War defeats Iraq; oil prices fall.

2003
US-led invasion and occupation of Iraq.

From 2003
Iraqi resistance groups attack oil installations.

2008
The soaring cost of oil causes economic problems worldwide.

2010
A forecast indicates that Iraqi oil production will quadruple within 10 years.

The USA and Iran

Iran is another country at odds with the USA. After an anti-Western Islamic government seized power in 1979, and Iranian students seized hostages at the US embassy in the capital Tehran, the USA broke off diplomatic ties with Iran and imposed economic sanctions. In the mid-1990s, it stiffened the sanctions. Then in the early 2000s, the USA grew concerned that Iran was making nuclear weapons, which it might use to harm US allies, such as Israel. Iran claimed that the nuclear programme was to produce energy.

▶ *Iranian President Ahmadinejad tours the Bushehr nuclear power plant in February 2006.*

Iranian oil exports

Since 2006, the UN has imposed economic sanctions against Iran because of its nuclear programme. Iran started to sell more oil to Asian countries instead. In 1995, 47 per cent of Iran's oil exports went to Europe and 23 per cent to Asia. In 2009, Europe took only 25 per cent while oil exports to Asia were 36 per cent. China is Iran's biggest market.

It emerged that the US government was considering military action against Iran, to stop it from developing nuclear weapons. Indeed, secret documents revealed by WikiLeaks in 2010 indicated that Saudi Arabia also wanted the USA to attack Iran, its rival power in the region.

Anti-war campaigners argued that the main issue was not nuclear energy, but that the USA would prefer a pro-Western Iranian government that would provide a reliable oil supply.

Enter China

The USA is not the only major player in international oil politics. China is the second largest oil consumer in the world and is increasingly dependent on Middle Eastern oil. By 2015, it is likely to source 70 per cent of its oil from the region. China is developing relationships with Middle Eastern countries, including selling arms to countries such as Iran, in return for access to purchase oil. This could create tension with the USA.

Viewpoints

'The other option for Obama is to look for triumph in foreign policy where he has a weak hand. The only obvious way to achieve success that would have a positive effect on the U.S. strategic position is to attack Iran. Such an attack would have substantial advantages and very real dangers. It could change the dynamics of the Middle East and it could be a military failure.'

George Friedman,
26 October 2010

'We now have a déjà vu situation [like in Iraq] in which the U.S. and its allies, prodded by Israel, demonize Iran as a threat to world security and accuse it of having a program to develop nuclear weapons. As with Iraq, the real aim is a regime change in Iran to set up a U.S. puppet government in this oil- and gas-rich country in the key strategic Persian Gulf region.'

Campaign Against Sanctions and Military Intervention in Iran (CASMII), 16 August 2010

• George Friedman is the chief executive of Stratfor, a global intelligence organization, and an expert on international affairs. He says that Obama's domestic policies are failing, so the 'other option' might be a war with Iran.

• CASMII is an independent organization that campaigns against sanctions, foreign interference and military intervention in Iran.

• Think about why each source might feel differently about US foreign policy towards Iran.

Oil-rich but divided

Oil is not only a source of international conflict. It has also created a divide within the oil-rich nations. The media often portray wealthy business tycoons from the Gulf States, buying up international companies and living in luxury. It is true that people in these states generally have decent living standards because their rulers have invested oil earnings in schools, hospitals and roads. Yet the riches are not shared out fairly. In Saudi Arabia, for instance, the ruling royal family siphons off much of the oil wealth to enhance its members' lavish lifestyle. This creates tensions within oil-rich Muslim countries, often expressed in religious terms. Many feel that their rulers' extravagant lifestyle is not true to the Islamic faith. The Prophet Muhammad taught that people should not keep more for themselves than they need.

Choke points

Most of the crude oil that is transported from its source is carried through relatively narrow shipping lanes and through pipelines. These are known as 'choke points' because it would be possible for a terrorist group to block one of them and obstruct the transport of oil. This is a constant concern for countries that rely on Middle Eastern oil.

Radical Islamic groups, such as Al-Qaeda, challenge Western military and economic intervention in the Middle East and also their own rulers. They threaten attacks on Western oil companies in the region to put pressure on the government to expel them. In 2010, fearing terrorist strikes, Saudi Arabia established a security force to protect its oil installations and arrested large numbers of suspected radicals.

▲ *Great wealth is on display in Dubai, United Arab Emirates.*

Viewpoints

'Shell has been in the Middle East [for] 100 years. We've been very successful working in every country in the Middle East over these years. In some cases we've been nationalized and told to leave. In some cases we've been invited back. We're currently working in the Empty Quarter of Saudi Arabia with Total [gas and power provider] trying to find gas in Saudi Arabia. We're ready to work in Iraq as soon as security and rule of law and the . . . invitation to work there comes, but we need all three. But ladies and gentlemen the Middle East needs attention. The Middle East needs resolution.'

John Hofmeister, 2006

'The sanctuaries, the assets and the wealth of the (Islamic) nation have been violated and spoiled by the heinous infidels [wicked non-Muslims] and their agents in the apostate [unreligious] governments.'

Al-Qaeda

• John Hofmeister served as president of the Shell oil company from 2005–08 and published a book in 2010 giving an insider's view of the petroleum oil industry.

• People linked to Al-Qaeda believe that non-Muslims have no right to the resources of Muslim countries. Owing to the secretive nature of the organization, the quote is not linked to a specific person.

• Who do you think should control the oil resources?

◄ *Police remove vehicles damaged in a clash with people suspected of being Al-Qaeda militants in Riyadh, Saudi Arabia, 2006.*

Chapter 6

Outlook for the future

The situation in the Middle East appears gloomy, with possibilities of further and wider warfare. Yet there is also the potential to heal the divisions over land, water and oil and for peaceful coexistence in the region.

Providing water

Climate change may increase the pressure on already scarce water resources in the region. By 2050, nearly 60 countries worldwide may face water shortages, including most Middle Eastern countries. Rich countries can afford expensive technologies to provide their population with a clean water supply. For example, the Gulf States and Israel have invested heavily in desalination plants. Another way to improve the situation is to promote water sharing. Water crosses national boundaries so it is vital to encourage co-operation. For instance, in 2010, nine north-eastern African countries were discussing how to share the waters of the River Nile.

Oil and renewable energy

The discovery and exploitation of oil in other regions could reduce pressure on the Middle East as an energy source and reduce friction between oil-hungry nations and their suppliers. However, the oil will run out one day, and the increasing use of fossil fuels is causing climate change. If dependence on petroleum decreased, there would be benefits to the environment and perhaps tensions would be eased, too.

Efforts are being made to promote renewable energy in the Middle East. In this hot, sunny region, using solar power is practical. In 2010, Tunisia announced 40 projects to develop solar power. Morocco aims to establish five solar generation sites, capable of producing 38 per cent of its electricity by 2020.

▼ *Photovoltaic solar panels provide electricity to a private home in the Bedouin Arab village of Darajat in Israel's Negev Desert.*

Abu Dhabi in the UAE is investing in the manufacture of photovoltaic (PV) cells – cells containing silicon crystals that produce electricity from the sun's rays. They are usually placed on a roof to catch the maximum amount of sunlight. PV cells are particularly effective in hot places.

Wind power is also being developed in some countries, including Egypt, Morocco, Tunisia and the UAE. Egypt has strong and consistent winds and in 2010 announced plans for a wind farm that would be one of the largest in Africa.

Renewable energy

• Several Middle Eastern countries, including Israel, Saudi Arabia, Kuwait, Bahrain and Qatar, have established desalination projects.

• In 2010, solar energy projects were announced in Egypt, Tunisia, Morocco, Algeria, Jordan, Saudi Arabia and the UAE.

• There is huge potential for the development of wind farms in the Middle East. Egypt plans to supply 12 per cent of its energy from wind power by 2020.

The peace process

As well as attempts to reduce the pressure on resources, direct efforts have been made since the 1970s to end the conflict between Israel and its Palestinian and Arab neighbours. The United States has led this peace process and has the greatest influence over its outcome. To date, it has not succeeded. Many Palestinians and Arab states, as well as Israeli historians critical of their government, argue that Israel does not want to make peace. Yet Israel maintains that it is the Palestinians and Arabs who refuse to negotiate.

Several sticking points prove hard to resolve. The territory could be divided, with Israel remaining a Jewish state within the 1967 borders, and a Palestinian state in the West Bank and Gaza Strip with East Jerusalem as its capital. This is known as the 'two-state solution.' However, Israel has extensive settlements in Greater Jerusalem and the West Bank. Also, there is the vexed issue of the Palestinian refugees. They want the right to return, but Israel does not agree to this.

Different kinds of solutions are possible. Israel is far stronger in terms of weapons and international support than the Palestinian authorities. It could potentially impose an unfair settlement, backed up with force. An alternative would require addressing the underlying historical issues to produce an agreement based on justice and the sharing of the land between the two peoples.

▲ *Israeli Prime Minister Benjamin Netanyahu shakes hands with Palestinian Authority Chairman Mahmoud Abbas, with US Secretary of State Hillary Clinton in the middle, during peace talks in September 2010.*

Case Study

The West-Eastern Divan Orchestra

In 1999, the Israeli conductor Daniel Barenboim and Palestinian scholar Edward Said established an orchestra for young musicians from Israel and various Middle Eastern Arab countries. They aimed to encourage cultural exchange between the participants. The orchestra meets for workshops every summer in Seville, Spain and the project also raises money for music education projects in Israel, the Palestinian territories and Spain.

The project leaders believe that the destinies of Israelis and Arabs are linked together. Music cannot solve the problems but can allow bridges to be built because Israelis and Arabs meet on an equal footing in the orchestra. As Israeli cellist Noa Chorin says, 'When I am playing next to Dana from Syria I don't think, "She's from Syria", I think, "That's my friend Dana." '

◄ *Israeli conductor Daniel Barenboim directs the orchestra, which is composed of Israeli, Palestinian and Spanish musicians, August 2003.*

Viewpoints

'The Arabs have repeatedly outstretched a hand to peace and Israel has always rejected it.'

Avi Shlaim, *Haaretz*, August 13, 2005

'It is clear today . . . that Israel wants peace – to enter the peace process with the aspiration of fulfilling it. I don't see the same firmness on the other side.'

Benjamin Netanyahu, 29 November 2009

• Avi Shlaim, writing in an Israeli newspaper, is an Israeli historian critical of the government.

• Netanyahu is Israel's Prime Minister, elected in 2009.

• Why do you think that there are such different viewpoints from Israelis?

Glossary

Al-Qaeda An Islamic terrorist network that wants US forces to leave the Middle East and to set up Islamic governments across the Muslim world.

aquifer A layer of rock or soil that can absorb and hold water.

blockade The act of surrounding or closing a place to stop people or goods from coming in or out.

checkpoint In the Palestinian territories, a place where people have to stop to allow Israeli soldiers to check their documents.

civil war A war between groups of people within the same country.

commando A soldier trained to carry out quick attacks in enemy areas.

communist Ruled like the system of government in the former Soviet Union, where the government owned and controlled the means of production, such as farms and mines.

concession Something that is offered to make a situation less difficult, for example, giving up land.

coup A sudden, illegal and often violent change of government.

Dome of the Rock The Muslim shrine (holy place) in Jerusalem, built over a sacred stone.

flotilla A group of boats sailing together.

Greater Jerusalem An area of approximately 100 square miles (about 250 sq km) around Jerusalem.

Gulf States The countries bordering the Persian Gulf in south-west Asia.

Hamas A militant Palestinian Islamic movement. Its short-term aim is to drive Israeli forces out of the Occupied Territories. In the long term, it aims to establish an Islamic state to replace Israel.

Hizbullah A powerful Islamic political and military organization based in Lebanon, which is hostile to Israel.

Islamist To do with the movement to revive Islam and bring Islamic values into all aspects of life.

Israel A country in the Middle East; around three quarters of the population are Jewish, while nearly a quarter are Arab.

militant Willing to use force or strong pressure to achieve social or political change.

nationalize When the government takes over the ownership of a company or industry.

non-governmental organization (NGO) An organization that is not part of government and does not make profits.

Occupied Territories The Palestinian land occupied by Israel after the 1967 war: East Jerusalem, the West Bank and the Gaza Strip.

Ottoman rule Rule by the Ottomans from Turkey. They ruled Palestine from 1517 to 1917.

outpost An unofficial Israeli settlement on the West Bank.

Palestine Liberation Organization (PLO) An organization founded in 1964 to fight for an independent state of Palestine.

Palestinian An Arab born in what was Palestine, or born to a family that comes from Palestine.

radical In favour of complete political or social change.

sanctions Measures imposed by a country or countries to restrict trade with another nation because it is behaving in an unacceptable way.

Security Wall/Separation Barrier A barrier to separate Israel from the West Bank, which Israel has built to stop Palestinians from entering Israel without permission.

terrorist A person who uses violent actions to achieve political aims.

tributary A stream or river that flows into a main river.

United Nations (UN) An organization founded at the end of World War II, with the aim of preventing future wars.

Western Wall According to Judaism, the only part of the ancient Jewish Temple in Jerusalem that still exists. It is a place of pilgrimage and prayer for Jews.

Timeline

1917 Britain conquers Palestine and establishes rule over it.

1947 The United Nations states that Palestine will be divided between the Palestinians and Jewish settlers.

1948 The State of Israel is founded.

1948–49 War between Israel and Egypt, Jordan, Syria, Lebanon, Iraq.

1950s Israel begins projects to divert surface water to its population.

1951 Iran nationalizes its oil resources.

1953 Prime Minister Mohammad Mossadeq of Iran is ousted in a US- and British-sponsored coup.

1960 The oil nations form the Organization of the Petroleum Exporting Countries (OPEC).

1964 Syria starts work on diverting river water away from Israel.

1966 Syria abandons its water-diversion plan.

1967 Israel conquers the West Bank, Gaza Strip, Golan Heights and the Sinai Peninsula during the Six-Day War. It takes over the West Bank's water resources.

1972 Iraq nationalizes its oil supplies.

1973 During the Yom Kippur War, Israel defeats a surprise attack by Syria and Egypt.

1973 OPEC raises oil prices for the countries that supported Israel in the Yom Kippur War.

1979 An Islamic government takes power in Iran.

1980–88 Iran–Iraq War. Between 500,000 and 1.5 million die.

1982 Israel invades Lebanon to crush the PLO.

1987–93 First Palestinian *intifada* (uprising) in the West Bank and Gaza Strip against Israeli rule.

1990 Iraq invades Kuwait and world oil prices rise.

1991 US-led forces attack Iraq in the Gulf War and restore the Kuwaiti government. Oil prices fall.

1993 The Palestinian Water Authority is created to give the Palestinians more control over their water resources.

1994 As part of the Jordan–Israel peace agreement, the two countries agree to co-operate over the management of water supplies.

May 2000 Israeli troops leave Lebanon.

September 2000 Second Palestinian *intifada* breaks out against Israeli rule. (No agreement on whether or not it has ended).

2001 Al-Qaeda terrorist attacks on the USA kill nearly 3,000 people.

2002 Israel starts building the Separation Barrier/Security Wall on West Bank land.

2003 The USA leads the invasion and occupation of Iraq, toppling the dictator Saddam Hussein.

From 2003 Iraqi resistance groups attack oil installations in Iraq.

2005 The Israeli government forces Israeli settlers to leave the Gaza Strip.

2006 The Islamist party Hamas wins the elections in Gaza.

2006 Israel invades Lebanon after the kidnapping of two Israeli soldiers.

2008 The soaring cost of oil causes economic problems worldwide.

November 2008 Israel invades Gaza in response to rocket attacks on its territory. Its military actions in Gaza leave Palestinians without tap water.

2009 Benjamin Netanyahu is elected Prime Minister of Israel.

2010 Saudi Arabia establishes a security force to protect its oil installations from possible terrorist attack.

Palestinians in the West Bank experience a severe water crisis.

Solar energy projects are announced in several Middle Eastern countries.

May 2010 Israeli commandos fight activists on a ship carrying aid to Gaza.

October 2010 The US government announces a plan to sell $60 billion (£38 billion) worth of weapons to Saudi Arabia.

Further information

Books

Access to History: Crisis in the Middle East: Israel and the Arab States 1945–2007 by Michael Scott-Bauman (Hodder Education, 2009)

Creation of the Modern Middle East: Israel by Louise Chipley Slavicek (Chelsea House Publishers, 2008)

Opposing Viewpoints: Israel by Myra Immell (Greenhaven Press, 2010)

The State of the Middle East: An Atlas of Conflict and Resolution by Dan Smith (Earthscan, 2008)

Websites

Btselem
http://www.btselem.org/English
Israeli human rights organization that aims to educate the public about human rights abuses in the Occupied Territories. It is critical of the Israeli government.

Israel4kids
http://www.israelemb.org/kids
Israeli embassy site about Israel, including relations between the USA and Israel. It gives the official Israeli government view.

Natural resources in the Middle East
http://www.pbs.org/wgbh/ globalconnections/mideast/ questions/resource/index.html
A US Public Broadcasting Service overview that gives a balanced view.

Water resources in the Middle East
http://go.worldbank.org/ B4UIMFFX60
An overview of water resources from the international finance organization, the World Bank.

Index